DRABBLE

MALL COPS, DUCKS and FENDERHEADS

By
KEVIN
FAGAN

NANTIER · BEALL · MINOUSTCHINE
Publishing inc.
new york

Also Available:
Son of Drabble: $9.95
One Big Happy: "Should I Spit On Him?", $9.95 (plus $3 P&H)
One Big Happy: "None Of This Fun Is My Fault!",$9.95

NBM has over 150 graphic novels available
Please write for a free color catalog to:
NBM -Dept. S
185 Madison Ave. Ste. 1504
New York, N.Y. 10016

ISBN 1-56163-216-3
©1998 United Feature Syndicate, Inc.
Printed in Canada

5   4   3   2   1

DRABBLE ® By KEVIN FAGAN

DRABBLE By Kevin Fagan

DRABBLE BY KEVIN FAGAN

DRABBLE. By KEVIN FAGAN

LATELY, WHENEVER DAD TRIES TO STAND UP, HE REMINDS ME OF A THEORY-OF-EVOLUTION CHART!

IT'S HECK BEING MIDDLE-AGED.

24

I FORGOT WHAT I CAME IN HERE FOR!!

THERE ARE THREE STAGES OF LIFE: YOUTH, MIDDLE AGE AND I-FORGOT-WHAT-I-CAME-IN-HERE-FOR.

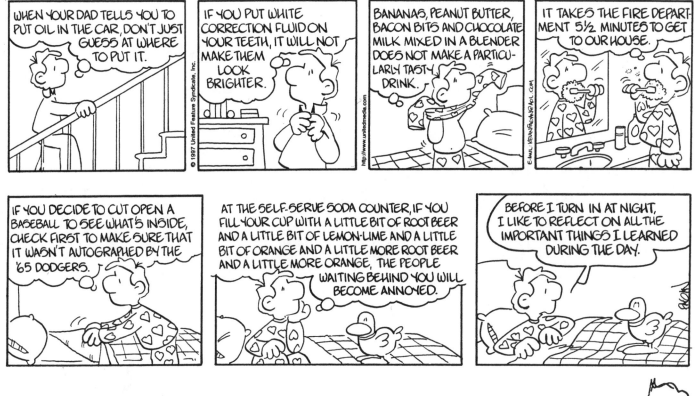

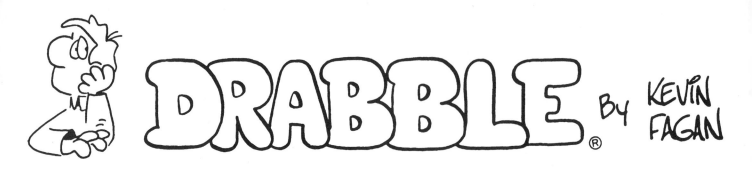

DRABBLE. BY KEVIN FAGAN

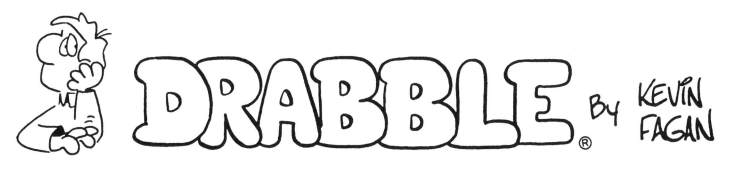

DRABBLE

By KEVIN FAGAN

Panel 1: DAD! COME HERE!! MY SEARCH FOR FOSSILS HAS FINALLY PAID OFF!!

© 1997 United Feature Syndicate, Inc.

Panel 2: I MAY HAVE STUMBLED UPON THE MOST IMPORTANT SCIENTIFIC DISCOVERY OF THE CENTURY! LOOK!!

E-MAIL: KFGNATE@AOL.COM

Panel 3: A BEEF RIB?

THAT'S WHAT I THOUGHT, TOO, BUT LOOK WHAT I FOUND RIGHT NEXT TO IT...

http://www.unitedmedia.com

Panel 4: A CHICKEN BONE?

EXACTLY! DO YOU KNOW WHAT THIS MEANS??

PAW PAW

Panel 5: IT MEANS THAT IN PREHISTORIC TIMES, OUR FRONT YARD WAS ROAMED BY A BIG COW-LIKE CHICKEN!

Panel 6: THESE DAYS, IT'S ROAMED BY A BIG TURKEY-LIKE HUMAN!

WOW! IT MUST'VE PLAYED GOLF, TOO!

DRABBLE. BY KEVIN FAGAN

Panel 1: Please write your account number on your check.

Panel 3: HEY, PATRICK, HOW MANY PEOPLE ARE THERE IN THE ENTIRE WORLD?

Panel 4: ABOUT 6,000,000,000

Panel 5: 6,000,000,000. NOW, THAT'S INTERESTING!

Panel 6: IF THERE ARE ONLY 6,000,000,000 PEOPLE IN THE ENTIRE WORLD, HOW COME MY CABLE TV ACCOUNT NUMBER IS 8073560111861016879148982691622562??

I'M STILL TRYING TO FIGURE OUT HOW THERE CAN BE 100 DIFFERENT CHANNELS, AND STILL BE NOTHING GOOD ON AT 8:30!

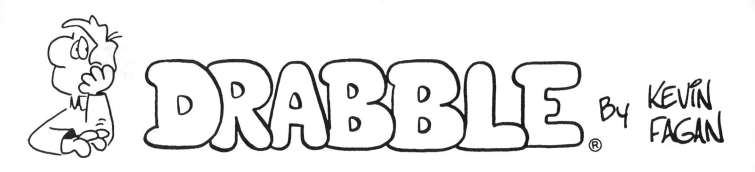

DRABBLE® BY KEVIN FAGAN

'BYE, NORM! HAVE A GOOD DAY AT SCHOOL!

OH, AND NORMAN?...

YEAH, DAD?

THE GLARE?? WHAT DID I DO TO DESERVE THE GLARE??

NOTHING.

BUT IF, DURING THE COURSE OF THE DAY, YOU'RE EVER TEMPTED TO DO ANYTHING THAT I MIGHT DISAPPROVE OF, JUST KEEP IT IN MIND!

I WILL!

OH, AND NORM? ONE MORE THING...

WHAT WAS THAT ONE FOR??

THAT WAS JUST AN INSURANCE GLARE!

89

DRABBLE. By KEVIN FAGAN

VARMINTS

FWEEEEEET!

GREAT GAME, VARMINTS! GREAT GAME!

EVERYBODY LINE UP, AND I'LL DISTRIBUTE THE POSTGAME TREATS!

REMEMBER, TAKE ONE PORK RIND EACH, THEN A DRINK FROM THE HOSE!

I HATE IT WHEN IT'S YOUR DAD'S TURN TO BRING THE SNACKS!

DRABBLE. BY KEVIN FAGAN

Panel 1: SO, WHAT WOULD YOU LIKE ME TO GET YOU FOR CHRISTMAS, HONEYBUNCH?

Panel 2: YOU HAVEN'T EVEN BOUGHT MY **CHRISTMAS GIFT** YET??

Panel 3: I BOUGHT **YOUR** PRESENT LAST **AUGUST!!**

Panel 4: I WAS FINISHED BUYING GIFTS FOR EVERY MEMBER OF OUR FAMILY BY **MID-OCTOBER !!!**

Panel 5: I WRAPPED EVERY SINGLE PRESENT, AND SINGLE-HANDEDLY SIGNED, ADDRESSED AND MAILED CHRISTMAS CARDS TO EVERY SINGLE PERSON WE KNOW, BY **LATE-NOVEMBER !!**

Panel 6: AND HERE IT IS, EIGHT O'CLOCK ON DECEMBER 22nd, AND YOU HAVEN'T EVEN **BOUGHT** ME ANYTHING YET ???

Panel 7: TELL YOU WHAT, RALPH: YOU'VE BEEN WORKING SO HARD, DON'T EVEN BOTHER TO BUY ME A GIFT!
WELL... OK!

Panel 8: THAT'S WHAT I LIKE ABOUT YOUR MOM— SHE'S SO EASY-GOING!
I HAVE HALF A MIND TO RETURN YOUR VALENTINE'S PRESENT!

© 1996 United Feature Syndicate, Inc.

http://www.unitedmedia.com

DRABBLE® BY KEVIN FAGAN

I'VE GOT YOU NOW! THERE'S NO ESCAPE!

AAAAAHHH!

© 1998 United Feature Syndicate, Inc.

Sigh..

OH, HI, DAD!

NORM, I DON'T GET IT... YOU'RE ALMOST 20 YEARS OLD! WHY CAN'T YOU ACT YOUR AGE?

THAT'S A GOOD QUESTION, DAD. I'VE GIVEN IT CONSIDERABLE THOUGHT, AND I THINK I KNOW THE ANSWER...

www.comiczone.com

I SLEEP EIGHT HOURS A NIGHT. THAT'S 1/3 OF MY LIFE THAT I'VE SPENT UNCONSCIOUS...

1/3 OF MY LIFE EQUALS ABOUT 6½ YEARS. I THINK IT'S FAIR TO SUBTRACT THOSE 6½ YEARS FROM MY AGE, SINCE I HAVE NO MEMORY OF THEM!

THEREFORE, EVEN THOUGH I'M ALMOST 20, IN REALITY, I'M ONLY ABOUT 13!

E-MAIL KEVINFFAGAN@AOL.COM

SO HOW COME YOU ACT LIKE YOU'RE SIX ??

DON'T FORGET... I'VE ALSO TAKEN QUITE A FEW NAPS!

112

121